Henry Reeves

Chimasia

A Reply to Longfellow's Theologian - And Other Poems

Henry Reeves

Chimasia
A Reply to Longfellow's Theologian - And Other Poems

ISBN/EAN: 9783744760775

Printed in Europe, USA, Canada, Australia, Japan

Cover: Foto ©Lupo / pixelio.de

More available books at **www.hansebooks.com**

CHIMASIA:

A

REPLY TO LONGFELLOW'S THEOLOGIAN;

AND

OTHER POEMS.

BY ORTHOS.

———

PHILADELPHIA:

J. B. LIPPINCOTT & CO.

715 AND 717 MARKET STREET.

1864.

CONTENTS.

CHIMASIA.

1*

CHIMASIA:

A REPLY TO LONGFELLOW'S THEOLOGIAN.

THE ride was long, the day was cold and wet;
My outer glove was ice; and nature set
Her kingdoms in a case of frozen mail.
The misty hills, that passed me within hail,
Were ice-clads, looming in a frozen sea;
They rode the storm, though hard it blew to lee.
Ill time it were for darkness to waylay,
With clinking branches swinging in the way,
And frequent from above, with startling sound,
The crash of limbs that thunder'd to the ground.
'Twas when the days were dwarf'd, like Esqui-
    maux,
And works were feeble, as in huts of snow.
More puny still upon that night of harm,
Seem'd all the doings of the creature's arm;
His goodness sank to zero, when from high
The winter solstice vex'd the earth and sky.

(7)

Cold sighs and freezing drops that round me
    swept,
Seem'd as the tears by heartless pity wept.

'Twas dark before the night; no inn was near,
To stay my steps with hospitable cheer.
Perhaps, I said, this lane, that seems to lead
To yonder light, may help a stranger's need.
Reserve forbids, but not to break the ice
May lose a shelter, or at least advice.

A farmer's house appear'd, begirt with trees,
With signs of thrift, mayhap of rural ease.
The owner, at the door, my form survey'd,
'Mid flickering shadows cold, with hand to shade
The light the winds would fain puff out. "My
    friend,"
Was his reply, "your case I comprehend.
Come in, and feel at home; the air is bleak;
Our supper will be ready soon; I speak
Your company to-night, too bad a night
To be abroad." When to the chimney bright
He drew me near, within the circle dear,
"An evil night," he said, " to some, I fear."

And then, by order prompt, my horse was led
Away to stable door, and housed and fed.
My thanks I speak, my blessing is unsaid,
But felt, withal, for him that bids me stay
Till fairer weather on the coming day,—
For her so cheerful and so debonair,
Who pleasant welcome makes in savory fare,—
For children well-behaved, with eyes so bright,
Their novelty a stranger guest to-night.
My blessing too was felt although unsaid,
When at the meal in thanks the father led.

Then, by the evening fire, my host I found
Of fair intelligence and judgment sound.
And books and facts and questions of the day
In quaint mosaic did his mind inlay.
With soul awake, a man upon the soil
May stores of knowledge gain despite his toil.
The while he plows, he turns the glebe of thought,
—Of thought in furrows long and deeply wrought.
The sage conclusion, slow, but doubly sure,
Well-earn'd, is all his own, and will endure.

When at my friend's behest I could but tell
My story too, it pleased the children well.

I turn'd to one, and, "Sonny boy," I said,—
The mother smiled,—declared I had betray'd
My fatherhood by "sonny boy," a word
From else than parent's lips she ne'er had heard.
My question ask'd, the boy the answer told
In catechism's phrase, all words of gold.
"Ah! now I see, my friend, and seeing bless
The source of such domestic happiness.
The Bible and its helps you here espouse;
You have foundations to your peaceful house."

When this I said, a wailing fury woke
The voiceful legions of the night, and broke
Upon the house in wrath, and shook its frame.
Amid the trees a fearful rushing came.
I thought 'twas he, the gospel-hating Thor,
With swinging sledge aloft and breathing war.
A tree was carried headlong, aud the blast
The mansion shook,—it did no more,—and pass'd.
Yet, as in mad regrets, the driving sleet
Upon the panes and weatherboarding beat.

"Ah! this is well," said I; "a wandering thing,
I coursed the stormy air with tired wing,

Escaped in time the strong and rueful night,
Within this dove-cot am I hidden quite.
The old world's tents of hospitality
Excel its high-wrought Pharos by the sea,
Its labyrinthine wonders, sphinxes, fanes,
And all the splendor rear'd on Theban plains.
In memory's ledger often will I turn
To where I credit you with this sojourn,
For entries, bearing interest, here begin ;
Item, his house became my wayside inn."

"Then write again," the farmer, smiling, said,
"Per contra, this has all in full been paid.
But, sir, your words remind me of a book
That pleased me much ;" and from a shelf he
      took
A book of Tales in verse, the Wayside Inn.
"Not many such my admiration win
So well as this, when taken all in all.
Your own opinion I would not forestall,
In begging leave to say, one part I take
With some exception for the gospel's sake.
In books I am not querulous, nor make

My neighbors' ears to ring when I have read;
A liker wide I am, as Allston said.
In quietude I like to take my page,
As patient kine enjoy their pasturage.
The bitter herb, though intermix'd, they pass,
In silence leave it, while they crop the grass.
But seated here, on winter evening bleak,
To wile the lingering hours we freely speak. (1)

"Sad is the Theologian's tale, and good; (2)
But in his sketch you find, and Interlude,
A tincture like a drop of gall in curds,
And better known by taste than told in words.
A young divine, with epidermis thin,
He cannot bear a sermon upon sin,
Nor threatenings of the last account allow,—
A Bible student too.   Beholding now.
A creed-betraying tilt at creed, expect
A raid sectarian on the plague of sect."

Then I remark'd, "The poet merits praise,
Whose verse against the bigot's brand inveighs.
But this divine goes further, and betrays
A spirit mettlesome in air of truth."

The farmer thus replied, "He does, in sooth.
How runs his creed?　'The deed, and not the
　　creed,'
I read, 'will help us in our utmost need.'
God says 'tis Faith, and he, the Knowing,
　　Works;
Perplexing doubt the common people irks;
Between the two they know not which to trust,
Or will they turn from both with like disgust?
This I unsay, and think he may succeed,
Since poets of the olden time did lead
The dead march of the nations, by the road
Of myths and idols, from the hills of God.
No thunderbolts in hand disgrace his Jove,
For his Olympian King is only love.
But hark! it thunders now, and havoc leaps
From yonder cloud, and man surviving, weeps,
And weeping prays, as if th' Almighty Sire
Had struck the blow, or ever speaks by fire!
Poor simpleton!　How deftly taken in
He must have been, by sermons upon sin!
O shame! that friends of light are cross'd with
　　these,
Preachers on sin, physicians on disease! (3)

"To say, Behold yon canting Pharisee!
I beat my breast,—why, that is charity.
To say, He thanks his God he's not like me,
But I am humble! that's humility.

"To boast of dove-like charity is cheap,
When Bigotry is bound and fast asleep.
The power were proof; meanwhile the loudest
　　claim,
As rogues' professions honest people shame,
May point suspicion of the latent flame.
You find some traces of the ancient curse
In current catch-words and embitter'd verse.
This Theologian and his sort, I fear,
Old Fagot being dead, could they but hear
Of advertising for the next of kin,
To gain a windfall, would at once come in."

"How soon," said I, "extremes come round
　　and meet.
Let Páris tell, dire Revolution's seat,
Where revel'd Anticreed in bloody street.
If Superstition has its cruel spoil,
So Doubt, when from the same it makes recoil.

I will not lift the veil; alike I fear
Their Torquemada and their Robespierre."

"This brings into my mind," the farmer said,
"A fact in point, and which you may have read.
There lately died in France an aged crone,
Beggar'd and blind, with reason overthrown.
Thus had she lived for twenty years and more.
Why lay this wreck so long upon the shore?
Behold the goddess Reason of poor France!
Strange! she it was—'tis stranger than romance—
Whom in those bloody days they took and
    throned,
An emblem of the only god they own'd. (4)
Come all ye wise who reason magnify
Beyond the voice that speaketh from the sky,
Look there! your goddess in the straw doth lie.
Gaze on the idiotic countenance,
And bow ye down to worship with poor France!
Ah, yes! the Galilean reigns; we see
There is a God,—at least in history."

"He speaks in lofty praise of deeds," said I;
"Great praise, if when we die, we may rely

Upon the merits of a life well-spent.
But say how far shall this command assent?"

Then answer'd he, "There was a certain tree,
And one was bought by each of neighbors three.
Old Mr. Legalist, with pick and spade,
A spacious hole to fit the branches made;
And then upturn'd his tree, and in the air
The withering roots spread out, grotesque and
    bare.
To him I said, Our gospel tree, my friend,
I see you have inverted, end for end,
And faith and all upon the law depend.
Young Antinomian set his tree upright,
Then straightway fell'd to earth its branching
    height.
I spare the root, I have no use, said he,
For all the spreading portion of the tree.
And then I said, If faith is all with him,
His root will be as dead as leaf and limb.
But Godwin's tree delightful fruitage bare,
Whose root was set aright with early care."

I said, "Like lady's hat on pictured card,
For which the whole she treats with no regard,

Once it was lovely, just at fashion's height,
But now the portrait is a horrid fright,
So works with which the man himself cajoles,
And all the millinery of little souls,
With customs changed, in awful change of state,
Will seem but profitless and out of date;
So ill they sit, the man appears the worse
With all his self-approval in reverse."

So talk'd we on; and when I took a light,
At nine, and we were parting for the night,
He gave me pen and ink, a sketch to write
Of this our theologian; it would be
A kept memorial of the night and me.

Within my room the signs profuse I find
Of ancient comfort, with the new combined.
The ten-plate answers to the tempest's roar,
And shows a heart of fire through little door.
I mark'd the bellows trim, the snuffer tray,
Blankets in strata, and a sampler gay.
High ran the chest of drawers, to seven or more,
The mirror grand a ship in picture bore;
While quilt of stars, and carpet on the floor

Betoken'd industry, and careful plans
Of woman's patience, far surpassing man's.
O grace of rural art and simple love!
Thou art a nation's hope and treasure-trove,
And not rich land or ore, much less the glare
Of proud saloon and storied marble square.
Maternal rooms, adorn'd by virtue's hand,
Send forth your sons to vote and rule the land!
Beneath your laws my portion may I take,
Nor wish for such as lordly schemers make.
Delaying thus a little while to note
The things about the room, I sat and wrote.

The merit-monger, with his string of deeds,
Who counts them as a cloister'd girl her beads,
May have a charm to gain the world's ap-
　　plause,　　　　　　　　·
But who can bolster up to heaven with straws?
No court will make the act the only fact,
But rather this, what color'd such an act?
The master may prefer the grafted fruit,
Which first among the angels had its root.
Look to the life,—its all-availing source;
Look to the life again,—its rightful course,

For laxer rules let flippant doubters chafe ;
The life whose source and course are right, is
    safe.

  But O to deeds awake, to deeds of love,
And say not, ask not, what they bring above.
If sorrow's hour is dark, enough to know
They bring a sunlift to this world below.
To hear, to read the touching incident,
As told by some on love's Commission sent,
In field, or hospital, or straiten'd home,—
To read with eyes unto the dew-point come,
And say, He had a father then,—or this,
His babes will weep; O what a world it is !
My treasure of a wife, how would she feel,
If it were she ? May God her sorrows heal !
Is well. But see ! a-message writ for you,
Heaven's perfume on it; here is work to do.
Go forth abroad, on works of mercy bent,
Make for yourself your tearful incident ;
'Tis waiting for you in the neighboring street,
God sent you in the world the same to meet;
Up ! morning breaks, and hear the reveille beat !

There is no standing with clasp'd hands and
    dress'd
In robes of white for heaven; there is no rest
Save in these ways of mercy; Him we see
When He can say, Thou didst it unto me.
The good within, O speed it; let it roll,
Till all subliming, it enwrap the soul.
Resistless passion doth the world require,
Calls for a seraph's living wheel of fire.
With this the fervent spirit overrides
The world's obstructions and its sluggish tides.
Passion bestirs the spheres around, if slow,
As Moscow burning moved the winds to blow.

From Polar seas an illustration take,
When, Franklin's fate unknown, our Kane would
    break
The ice-lock'd secret of the North, he sail'd
Where Argonauts of weaker nerve had quail'd,
To the pole-dragon's jaws of night and cold,
That closed upon him, and their prey did hold.
At first the men their daily prayer address,
"Accept our thanks, our undertaking bless."

The summer pass'd, the irksome winter came,
Their daily prayer of thanks was still the same.
Bright moons revolve, and still the ship doth lie,
Lock'd in the ice, as pupil in the eye.
And oft the stars and north-light ceased to glow,
That heaven might weave for them a shroud of
 snow.
Their sanguine hopes are fled, their task is o'er;
Homeward they look, nor pray they as before,
But thus entreating, to the altar come,
"Accept our thanks, and send us to our home."

So we our hearts in grateful mood maintain,
For life's unselfish aims and toils humane.
The work we prize the more, the bounty less,
And daily ask, Our undertaking bless,—
Take heart the season in and out, and wait
Till brought by will of Heaven to helpless strait.
And when we see the stern and starless skies
Prepare the grave of human enterprise,
And life's surroundings, cast in icy mould,
Point upward with a ghostly hand and cold,
Where spirits stand, and beckon us to come,
We pray, and not till then, O take us home!

O Theologian, when I hear you preach,
Your words are changed before my ear they
    reach !
Or else it is their double, floating past,
"The practice, and the practice, first and last."
Until we see the needful doing done,
We cannot think your wings are fairly won,
Nor can we yet resign you to the sun.
Know you "the passing of the beautiful feet"
On distant mountain-top, and pagan street?
Say, have you gain'd a single ocean isle,
Or had one mission all this solemn while?
One swarthy youth the college sent, 'tis true,
But not till Asia sent him first to you.
Converted, to his Indian home he sail'd,
A Christian mission tried, and sadly fail'd.

The noblest field, the noblest working plan,
Include "all nations," nor omit a man.
Not mountain ranges, tidal seas or sounds,—
The planetary spaces are their bounds.
A world of four was all too large for Cain;
Not large the world to-day for souls humane.

To lend a hand to speed the world's uplift
In light to dry, all dripping from the drift
Of death,—to give it knowledge, laws, and thrift,
Is worthy work for man; for highest good
Doth run to all things, freedom, fire, and food.
If Christendom is better than the rest,
The will that all were Christendom is best.

O leave to ignorance to prattle thus,
"The Bible is a creed enough for us."
Were Nature's teachings answer'd so, the mind
Of man were dim, in science nearly blind.
The Book of Nature, read and labor'd o'er,
Is but the parent of a thousand more;
And those are next to God, though work of man,
Which best and briefest state the wondrous plan.
When blooming text-books grow on trees, when
      skies
Are letter'd o'er with sage astronomies,
Our Bibles too may fragrant blossoms bear,
And branching catechisms scent the air,
And little books unfold their leaves, and tell
The substance sweet, the system passing well.

But no! within the Word the science lies,
Just as we find it in the earth and skies.
And shall we leave it there?   The truth re-
plies,
The man who seeks me out I render wise.
He knows whereof he speaks, in nature's laws,
And laws divine, who thence the system draws.

How hard for those who error propagate
Its form in clear and naked terms to state!
But truth defined, or by the mirror laid,
Of its own likeness never is afraid.
Have little creed to match opinions small,
And do without if you have none at all.
If nothing you believe, not even Amen,
Your faith will never tax a tongue or pen.
If something, say so; make it clear and brief;
Let churches do the same with their belief,
And churches of the churches; for all else
Is trickery, *suppressio veri*, shells
With fuse and sawdust in, and sacred stalls
For Trojan horses brought within the walls,
And o'er the tree of life the wormy pest,
The infidel, encroaching with his nest.

The foe to spoil the church would make essay,
By taking her defences first away;
Not for the curtain is the blow design'd,
But for th' unloved Polonius behind.
And friends who would not break, but rather
    make
The church, there are, who blame her in mistake.
No spot was that they stoop'd to brush away;
Deceiving sunshine on her garment lay.

Transcendent gem in Zion's perfect crown,
Blest unity, from realms above come down!
And in thy coming, in the latter days,
Let old confessions share a meed of praise.
They kept the reckless plowshare from the field,
And oft a real unity reveal'd.
Like drops that by-and-by together run,
The sects, though many, are in substance one.
Each drop we leave itself to mould, and see
How well, when self-express'd, the most agree.
Behold, in ages past, in trace obscure,
A Christian people in the faith endure.
Ah, well for coming time, their creed they write;
Their course is run, they vanish out of sight.

And loosely now no foes their name malign;
Thank God, before they died they made a sign,
A sign that all who see have understood,
Whereby they rank in Christian brotherhood.

Ye wise, who sects decry with grievance sore,
And so withdraw, and form one sect the more!
Here hangs a portrait; there, with rarer art,
Looks down a larger one; from next my heart
I this unclasp;—in all see Washington.
They differ, as you see; but they are one.
We know him, love him, and esteem him great,
Though young, or militant, or magistrate;
Or standing, sitting, kneeling.   Here the vest
You can but notice; *that* is plainly dress'd;
And each has charms not portion'd to the rest:
Thus is it with the image of the Blest.
As features may be varied without end,
One photograph will not present your friend;
But many image forth the soul; and one
You like the best; but know you that the sun
Can tell no lies, though some are not well done.
Thus to the churches of our Lord are given
Some likeness to their head by light from heaven.

Smitten alike the guilty and the good,
What more have these if those the wrath elude?
Or how the wrong in present life amend,
If death is like to all, and heaven the end?
Shall not the foes that clinch'd in wrath expire,
The seats dispute in chariot of fire?
Our heaven is turn'd to one Valhalla vast,
Without the festal trump's reviving blast.
Admitted to the cage, the hectoring jay
With feathers raised, the linnet sweet will slay.
The maiden meets a phantom, just arrived,
And all th' unburied horrors are revived;
With hands imploring, from the man she flies,
And panting, Let me out of heaven! she cries.
Your Torquemada there will light his fire,
And prophets turn to stone around the pyre.
The old Hidalgo, to his nature true,
His hunting cry of blood will there renew,
Till golden streets sink down plutonic stone,
"Kill! kill! and let the Lord find out his
    own!" (5)

High in Mohammed's heaven their names they
    carve,
Who glut the wish and let the conscience starve.

No creature lives, for noble wildness famed,
But by starvation may at last be tamed.
When conscience pines, nor wonted instinct
    heeds,
The victim follows where the master leads.
Perverted nature towering hopes will build,
On rising fumes from dreamy drugs distill'd.
The doting spirit cleaves the balmy skies,
Where light was born, and sails in ecstasies,
Where glory pours abroad its seven streams.
Is it for dreams to know themselves as dreams?
Then from its torpor bid the soul awake;
'Tis not unkind, with heaven and all at stake.
When blows a wind to rasp the mountain side,
Cold, as if pity from the earth had died,
And two are struggling with the drifted snow,
If hearts will beat, and blood consent to flow,
One sinks and feels no pain; akin to stone
He begs this only,—to be let alone.
His friend who knows the only hope, will hear,
And still denying, though it seem severe,
Perforce will rouse him up against his pleas.
'Tis better thus than let him lie at ease,
Yield to the soothing dream of life, and freeze.

So self-deception pleads, so truth alarms,
Till death, outdone, remits his subtle charms.

Then from fatigue, or lull'd by beating rain,
I fell asleep.   I thought I was in Spain,
And saw Don Quixote and a motley train,
And heard a priest address the valiant knight,
Who blush'd by turns the shades from red to
  white.
The priest complain'd; his friend and he werc
  stripped
But yesterday by galley slaves, unwhipt
Of justice, arrant thieves, and running free,
Thanks to a rash, mistaking clemency.
A knight had freed them, brave, but in the main
As great a rogue as they, or else insane.
For who would loose the wolves among the
  sheep,
Or let the foxes mid the poultry leap,
Or wasps let fly in honey?   Who but knew
Such work defrauded justice of its due?

A shuffling noise, and voices in the street;
And see! by chance a score of people meet;

3*

The pillars of a "liberal" church convene,
One sect they come, but not one sex, I ween,—
Doctors who draw and deacons who digest,
And lady speakers, angels unrepress'd,
But never unawares, for words attest,
With message masterly and self-confess'd.
From commonplace, the theme is soon the
    church ;
And like the waters at Bethesda's porch,
The troubled current of discourse doth flow,
And bubbles to the surface come and go.
What shall we do, they ask, for Zion's thrift?
Our church declining, needs a mighty lift.
How few, alas ! and growing less, says one :
In church-extension nothing have we done.
Another adds, Ah, well-a-day ! the gales
That heaven sends us, somehow miss our sails.
Another voice,—Your strictures are severe ;
The case is better, sirs, than doth appear.
Our influence has its measure and its sphere
Beyond the limits proper of our sect,—
Excuse the word,—whose reach is indirect
Among the doubting class and all the foes
Of Bibliolatry.　When all compose

One brotherhood, its numbers who can tell ?
'Tis ours to modify the infidel.
A few ! dear sir, the curb is not the well.
'Tis like the berg, from Greenland glacier torn,
And southward on the Arctic current borne ;
For while the drift is sailing all aglow,
Nine times its bulk is dragging on below.

We need, another mourns, more heart within.
We all have head enough,—so has a pin.
If so unlike the sects, we soon expire ;
We are a lump of ice in sea of fire. (6)
To gain the needful thawing at the heart,
Let us go back, and take another start.
Were meetings often held, and feelings stirr'd,
Revivals might ensue,—excuse the word.

A cautious clergyman rejoin'd : You know
We tried that artifice awhile ago.
We thought, as now, that Boston was a hive
Of creeping bees acold, and half alive,—
A monument of art, sublime, but chill,
Impassive as the stones of Bunker Hill.

And then the bells rang out, and overhead,
The dead! the dead! Awake and live! they
    said.
Awake to something heartsome, positive;
The dead! the dead! they said. Awake and
    live!
And so we preach'd as storming a redoubt,
And pounded on the books till dust flew out,—
Or tried to preach, but, hamper'd by our creed,—
Excuse the word,—how hard it was to plead
For the metempsychosis of the law,
And gospel's rationale with eclat!
Lo, a revival! thus it went abroad,—
Our ice-bound church at last is being thaw'd.
And then it all went down,—the crust was thin,—
Like Tibb's show window, when the horse went
    in.
'Tis not for me to counsel such a course;
The stream can rise no higher than its source.
For consecration and a soul of fire
A bland theology can ne'er inspire.

A woman speaks: I differ from you all;
I like the mode of cure electrical.

The ailment of the church is but a loss
Of her polarities, from left across
To right, but very much from head to foot,
As pointing upward to the absolute,
In our philosophy, or down to sense.
Let me explain : in systems, if propense
To hold th' electric fluid in excess,
In any part, or if they hold it less
Than nature gave, the consequence is pain.
The cure is simple, saturate or drain,
Just as the case may be. Of late the streams,
The church's life, have tended to extremes.
One type has settled in the low routine
Of deeds, philanthropy, and things terrene.
The other, soaring upward, gathers fire
From trains of meteor sparks as they expire.
The purest reason is their atmosphere ;—
You smile ; of course I mean a dozen here,
Myself included. Privileged, they love
To view the Vast, the Infinite, above,
Around, within, below, the God inwove ;
For Mind is God, and Nature's every line
Is he ; my little finger is divine.
But some of us too much to this incline.

These inflammations, in the head and feet,
Demand a remedy,—we must deplete.
O could the church but touch a living wire,
To pour from head to heart galvanic fire !
O could the feet electric force impart,
To help the vital regions of the heart !
I see it now ! to me the way is clear;
And let me say, because I have your ear,
Good friends, a weekly paper I propose,
Myself the editor; 'twill mend the flows
Electrical, and answer our desire;
The Battery of Life its name ; the wire
Shall be the circulation; give us here
Your names,—the price, three dollars by the year.

No one responding, in a dolorous strain
A deacon took upon him to complain :
The times are changed, I think; our deeds are
          poor,
Compared with those of Puritans of yore.
As toys that come apart by Christmas night,
Made up with mercenary oversight,
Our moral enterprises do not hold
Like those of Christians in the days of old.

They want, perhaps, a soul in the intent,
Or gracious mortising, or love's cement.

To this a preacher bows polite assent :
We're dying with excess of light, we paint
In tints not fit for sinner but for saint.
As God dispenses here both joy and grief,
So there some hell we need, just for relief.
For pictures must have shade as well as light,
And plants not day alone require, but night.
Some darkly-shaded background must be had,
Some gulf of brief despair —— O that's too bad !
The most reply.   And yet no way is found
To pry the vessel from the shallow ground.
And once again they cry, What shall we do,
Our hopes to raise, our fortunes to renew ?
When lo, a voice, but not from out the skies,
Come to the Wayside Inn, and advertise !

And then, — for dreams from scene to scene
        will glide,—
In lumbering coach among the hills we ride.
The wheels were stopping when a runner cried,

Unstrap your baggage at the half-way house,
That leads you to the glacier heights of Strauss.

   I will, I said ; and stopping there awhile,
I wander'd forth, the morning to beguile.
A dream will lightly sport with time and space,
But still I linger'd at a watering-place.
The walks were those that skirt the dizzy falls
Of vast Niagara, whose rocky walls
Some trees o'erhung, bedeck'd with shining
     sleet,
From rising mist that veil'd the plunging sheet.
Into the mist I look'd, and, far below,
Appear'd a ghostly shape, ascending slow.
The face was Kant's.   Another follow'd close,
And lo ! a third, a fourth, in shadow rose. (7)
Great genii of the mist, I saw them freeze
Their souls away upon the shining trees.
Then from the trees the sweetest sounds were
     blown,
Like many little bells of softest tone.
Come up ! come up ! for here is light, they
     chimed.
By light and music lured, the tree I climb'd,

And higher went, and sought the outer limb
That overhung the vortex, wild and dim.
Then snapp'd the branch; the bells to laughter
    broke,
And falling in a glittering shower, I woke.

At breakfast, o'er the omelette and toast,
My dreams amused my entertaining host,
And thereupon my paper must be read ;
And so conversing, we resumed the thread
We dropp'd the night before. And when he
    said,
"The poet, sir, for Hiawatha famed——"
" No more, I beg," the gentle wife exclaim'd ;
" I cannot bear to hear the poet blamed.
O had you seen, as I of late did see,
A card of lovely buds, his daughters three,
You would not have the heart to criticise."
Then told their names, what hair, what beaming
    eyes ;
Described them as alone a woman can,
Till led by tenderness we love the man.
Now I had often seen the group,—and more,
The very same trefoil my pocket bore ;

I drew it forth, my thoughtlessness confess'd,
" Madam, 'tis as you say, a sweet protest."
The pleasure felt, the children in our view,
Illumines all.   And then we turn anew,
And find the " Children's Hour," and read it
      through.

And when I took my horse, and bade adieu,
At every turn what beauty met my view !
O ne'er before did sun from cloudless sky
Behold so oft his image multiply.
Appear'd the orchard trees as hills of light,
And even stubble lovely to the sight.
In rock and fence, in barn and dwelling-side,
What earthly was did heaven's enamel hide.
The sleet for plunder'd leafage makes amends,
And wondrously attired, the forest sends
Greeting unto the meadows, where the blades
Are sheath'd in crystal, link'd with shining
      braids.
Thou wooded swamp ! 'tis not for me to pry
Thy depths within, more fitting druid's eye,
And trace each weird device of sorcery.

Through such a scene I pensive pass'd, nor
    knew
What hours were gone, till near the town I drew.
And then I saw the telegraphic lines
Were heavy with their rows of comb-like spines;
Each curve was an aurora, come by day,
That bent and shot its rays the other way.

O city beautiful, in bridal white!
Damascus yields to thee, with luster dight;
No streets invite with such a wealth of trees,
No Oriental suburbs equal these.

Around, it seem'd two suns upon us shone,
More silvery and soft the newer one.
Perhaps 'twas this that to the fable led,—
The fable old,—wherein the sun did wed.

Then one came up, a miner from his birth,
Who ne'er had seen the beauty of the earth;
Entranced, he thought his spirit glorified,
And kneeling, ask'd, When was it that I died?

Long avenues of trees without a shade;
White arches tall of graceful branches made;

Cathedral tracery 'twixt earth and sky,
Nor need of windows stain'd, and pointing
    high.

A crystal palace finish'd in a night,
With mystic dome of blue, and rose, and white,
With chandeliers and brilliants hanging free,
And cedars, thick with green-white tapestry.

O blessed meteor, that embosoms all!
From mansions bright, and glittering ice-drops
    small,
From galaxies renew'd with every tree,
A promise comes, of glory yet to be.

Unconscious all, we waited for the spring,
Not dreaming winter a new world would bring,
Nor aught suspecting, in the darksome night,
That morn would open all the gates of light.

Still onward! where upon the slanting way,
A sun that might enliven Chaos lay;
And sunward, up! through glory incident,
That with the firmamental glory blent.

So might the ladder Jacob saw have shone,
So track of angel host to Bethlehem flown.
Light fall the hoofs upon the pearly floor,
Exulting speed we up to heaven's door.

Why, Sleet divine! cried I, with swelling heart.
Was I not made in thee to bear a part?
Of thee all nature dead is but the wick;
O why the dead alone, and not the quick?

Then folly fled; I trembled at the thought;
And recollected now the ruin wrought.
The hill-top gain'd, I paused, and look'd around,
And saw where mangled willows strow'd the
      ground.
The icy blast had kill'd like furnace breath,
And even little buds were glazed in death.
O thus it takes a lifetime oft to pay
For fading joys, the glitter of a day. (8)

To what presumption is a mortal given
In putting spurs to pride to scale yon heaven!
And then I saw that frost and doubt were one,
And sleet was pantheistic doubt, whose Sun,

4*

Supreme, it sees in all things, great and small,
That transcendental glare, of God in all.
Cold unto death it is; give me a clod
To know and worship,—or a personal God.
It crushes hope; its desolation drear
Prevents the fruitage of th' eternal year.
Its fascinations ardent souls entice
To lie, bright insects, bedded in the ice.
No nests are tended in the icy grove,
No songs of praise to God and gentle love.
I seem'd to hear the branches on the street
Cry, as I pass'd, What is the use of sleet?

A truce to themes polemic on the lyre,
For what poetic thought can such inspire?
A shining wonder out of element,
A poet lies, to church disputes attent.
No claim have I; and mine no winged steed;
He never lost his wings to fight at creed.
The *odium theologicum* for grain
Makes Rosinantes of our horses twain.
The greater folly mine, the time to spend
In riding forth, the windmills to defend.
At greater risk of neck the poet tilts
Than I; his horse is shod with higher stilts.

Our first and ruling bard ! a serious thing
It is, I know, to controvert the king.
But when a king gets down on all his fours,
Even a child may ride him o'er the floors;
And all will laugh, and none the worse shall be;
For though he rend his garment at the knee,
What to a king is that, with plenty more,
And robes of state beside, a shining store?

O when you sing in your accustom'd strain,
Delighted, I am at your feet again,
For sweet you make my world, like summer rain.
And as your superscription 's writ thereon,
My heart returns, its roving wish foregone.
Such things reflected are in memory's stream,
So bright and beautiful, and like a dream
One longs to dream again, that from the past
Come golden links of verse, and bind me fast.
As is the well-known voice to lover's heart,
Allaying with its tones the trivial smart,
Your tuneful accents snatch away my soul,
And all I took I give you back in dole.
Spring's fairest flowers to you I bring, and strow,
Where melts away my wintry wreath of snow.

Full glad I see 'twas not the kingly arm
Of Saul that would the Lord's anointed harm,
But spirit not his own ; nor need he call
For stranger's harp his mind to disenthrall ;
His strains the surest medications prove,
Who wakes the world to harmony and love.

NOTES.

(1) page 12. A good-natured reply to those verses of Longfellow's late poem which come in contact with the doctrines of that class, respectable in numbers, generally denominated orthodox, will not be deemed a breach of the charity so justly commended in the Theologian's part; for the right to attack implies a right to defend. Equal liberty is all that is asked. The Theologian,

"from the school
Of Cambridge on the Charles,"

who comes before us as a pattern in morals and religion, is not dealt with unreasonably if his claims are canvassed, and his credentials examined. And in performing this duty we ought not to confine ourselves to the Theologian's words, but may be allowed to extend our range, rambling excursion though it be, to his associations.

(2) page 12. For sketch of the Theologian, see the Prelude to Tales of a Wayside Inn. The Interlude is that preceding the tale Torquemada.

(3) page 13. The better to illustrate these remarks of the farmer, and to explain subsequent allusions, an extract from the Theologian's Interlude may be given.

"And most of all thank God for this:
The war and waste of clashing creeds
Now end in words, and not in deeds,
And no one suffers loss, or bleeds,
For thoughts that men call heresies.

"I stand without here in the porch,
I hear the bell's melodious din,
I hear the organ peal within,
I hear the prayer, with words that scorch
Like sparks from an inverted torch,
I hear the sermon upon sin,
With threatenings of the last account.
And all, translated in the air,
Reach me but as our dear Lord's prayer,
And as the Sermon on the Mount.

"Must it be Calvin, and not Christ?
Must it be Athanasian creeds," etc.   *   *   *
"I know that yonder Pharisee
Thanks God that he is not like me;
In my humiliation dress'd
I only stand and beat my breast,
And pray for human charity."

(4) page 15. "One of the ceremonies of this insane time stands unrivaled for absurdity, combined with impiety. The doors of the convention were thrown open to a band of musicians; preceded by whom, the members of the municipal body entered in solemn procession, singing a hymn in praise of liberty, and escorting, as the object of their future worship, a veiled female, whom they termed the Goddess of Reason. Being brought within the bar, she was unveiled with great form, and placed on the right hand of the president; when she was generally recognized as a dancing girl of the opera, with whose charms most of the persons present were acquainted, from her appearance on the stage, while the experience of individuals was farther extended. To this person, as the

fittest representative of that reason whom they worshiped, the national convention of France rendered public homage."—*History of Modern Europe, by Wm. Russell, continued by William Jones*, vol. iii. p. 295.

(5) page 27. The reader will find a description of the "funeral fire," with statues of Hebrew prophets at the four corners, and of the cruel part the Hidalgo played, in "Tales of a Wayside Inn," article Torquemada.

(6) page 31. In a Unitarian assembly in New England a few years ago, about the time of "the revival" which the next speaker describes, a divine, deploring the low state of religion, and urging new plans of effort to promote the vitality of the church, used this language, "We are a lump of ice in a sea of fire."

(7) page 36. The four great philosophers of the German school are Kant, Fichte, Schelling, and Hegel, whose philosophical fictions received the homage of the German mind in the order here named.

Kant, (1785,) with a new system of philosophy, brought in a new religion, if that may be so called which has the heart and fiber of religion left out. We find him teaching that the human reason is self-sufficient and infallible, and we follow him to obscure heights and among clouds, but he shows us little place for God.

Fichte (1792) held that whatever exists out of the mind, the mind itself creates. All things center in one little word, I; from the I all things proceed. This system is a splendid egotism, a fit image of which is a man standing between two mirrors, beholding himself reflected indefinitely, sight without end.

Schelling (1814) taught that the soul and the objects of its thought are one and the same, and that the universe is God, who is ever revealing himself therein. God is a principle, not a person, and man is as infinite as any other being.

And lastly, (1818,) Hegel taught the same revolting doctrines of pantheism, with modifications of his own. He held that in the human reason is the highest manifestation of God. Whatever it be that thinks in us, that is God. Therefore there is no evil in sin. Finally, he proves that everything is nothing, that nature, man, God, are nothing!

These teachings appear reasonable enough to many. This is a brief glimpse of transcendentalism, and the above are a few points in the shining network that has taken captive many fine minds in Europe and America.

(8) page 41. The sleet-storm observed by the writer the week before Christmas, 1863, would defy, for beauty and destructiveness, poetical description. In the following May, when traversing a forest of pines upon a ridge of slate land, a singular scene opened to his view, the effect of this remarkable storm. In one spot a hundred pines might be seen, killed by the blast, some uprooted, others broken, but most of them bent to the earth, like praying Moslems hopelessly fixed in the posture of worship. And when the sleet comes to awaken mingled feelings of regret and admiration, long will it be ere old men will cease to tell of the Chimasia, the winter storm of 1863.

MISCELLANEOUS.

.

THE TRAPS VISITED.

INSCRIBED TO J. B. P.

A PEBBLE smites the window pane,
    And naught but glassy sleep it breaks ;
Th' expectant lad springs up amain,
    And dressing but a moment takes.
The stars all other stars surpass ;
    A greater charm than sleep is on,
Though late October chills the grass,
    And day has not begun to dawn.

A bluff salute when first they meet ;
    " Old boy " is seated on the trap,
And whistling to the gloomy street,
    While on the lid his fingers tap,—
A sort of boyish fife and drum,
    The waning spirits to recruit,
Or goblin spirits, ere they come,
    With tricks of daring to confute.

They stand and wonder why a star,
    A shadow casting, brightly burns ;
Then trudge away to woods afar,
    The trap on shoulder borne by turns.
If painters then had bodied forth
    Their little world, without, within,
What rabbits in the air and earth
    Around the trappers twain had been !

And now, the journey nearly done,
    No more they talk of shooting stars ;
The east is tinctured with the sun ;
    Its buried wealth in silver bars
Comes forth, and ruby skylights seem
    To be implanted far below,
That brightness through them up may stream,
    While wells of spléndor overflow.

O life, how bright ! thy morning sweet
    For freshness all the rest excels ;
The man doth chase the glory fleet
    That all unsought with childhood dwells.
But age shall find it at the last ;
    In childhood's border-land, the strain,

That linger'd from the ages past,
 The age to come shall hear again.

Their hearts with rare excitement bound,
 As deep within the bushy wild,
From box to snare they go the round,
 To find what prey has been beguiled.
The ground for other snares they clear;
 The gaping traps they bait anew,
And lie conceal'd what time they hear
 From neighboring woods a loud halloo.

The shadows fainter by degrees,
 The leafy walk, the distant chime,
The tread of moss, the scent of trees,
 Were things not treasured at the time.
And yet the breath of spruce and pine
 In later years restores the scene,
Wherever colors deck the vine,
 And autumn's path is evergreen.

THE SHOVEL SONG.

O HAD not nature made the ground
  For man, a little wrong,
No merry diggers would be found
  To sing the shovel song.
Then dig away, O Patrick, dig,
  And sing, O Patrick, sing!
There's dirt enough for all, dear friends,
  For dirt's the cheapest thing.

The breastwork stands with flag on high,
  And takes the iron rain;
The cannon on the hills reply
  In laughter to the plain.
Then dig away, O soldier, dig,
  And sing, O soldier, sing! etc.

If none should die in all the land,
  Too many there would be,
And some would find no place to stand,
  But slip into the sea.

Then dig away, O sexton, dig,
 And sing, O sexton, sing! etc.

The miner sings by candlelight,
 If any luck befall;
The gold is fine, and silver's bright,
 But iron's best of all.
Then dig away, O miner, dig,
 And sing, O miner, sing! etc.

When all our diggings have been clear'd
 And all our fences made,
Our country's greatness will be rear'd
 With shovel and with spade.
Then dig away, O farmer, dig,
 And sing, O farmer, sing!
There's dirt enough for all, dear friends,
 For dirt's the cheapest thing.

THE OLD BANNER GRAND.

WHEN flies apart the mountain chain,
  When flows no more the river,
Our country may be cleft in twain,
  Our flag be rent forever.
The locomotive leaps the line,
  And leaves the bands of iron;
The flag by art and nature strong,
  Is not the flag to fire on.
    Then take again, old banner grand,
      Our oath of true devotion;
    And take forever all the land,
      From ocean unto ocean.

The nation is a network grand;
  The state, apart, and banish'd
Is but the mesh within a net,
  When all the strings have vanish'd.

Your single stars, the sons of Mars
   Divide with one another ;
No foe can come within the bars
   When brother stands with brother.
     Then take again, old banner grand, etc.

The states are glass, the nation brass,
   With extra ribs of iron ;
The wandering star of upstart flags
   Is just the star to fire on.
Your single star the dogs of war
   Will take, then hunt another.
What earthly forces stronger are
   Than brother leagued with brother ?
     Then take again, etc.

Our banner brave the army bore,
   George Washington commanding ;
The state that dares the same to lower
   Will raise it, notwithstanding.
Then Washington's old flag unroll,
   For Union,-and forever !
Secession shames his noble soul,
   Undoing his endeavor.
     Then take again, etc.

Columbia's stars, in other wars
  Shone out, forever brightening;
Whoever climbs to strike the stars
  May come too near the lightning.
The southern breezes miss'd the flag,
  And northward they were blowing;
No more they rove,—the stars they love
  O'er southern heights are flowing.
    Then take again, old banner grand,
      Our oath of true devotion;
    And take forever all the land,
      From ocean unto ocean.

COME NOT.

COME Rest! with thirst untold
  Our souls for thee are pining;
Come, promise sweet of old,—
  The beasts of war reclining.
      Rest from the blade,
      From wreck and raid,
  But not *this* rest, Disunion!

Come Pain! wherein the heart
  With sorrow wrings and quivers,
In battle mine, the smart
  Which my dear land delivers.
      Come pain to me,
      If need must be,
  But not this pain, Disunion!

Come Shame, and shun the light
  With burning eyelids drooping,
The cheerful spirit's blight,
  To death ignoble stooping.

Come, flying fame,
Eclipse my name,
But not this shame, Disunion !

Come Death ! and bid me dare
Thy labyrinthine portals,
Without the gloss and glare
That blind the eyes of mortals ;
The terror wild
Of grieving child ;
But not this death, Disunion !

Come, fail me not, my love,
Thou map of states before me,
Hung here, but drawn above,
Picture of land that bore me !
My love may die,
And buried lie,
But not this love, the Union.

LOOK UP.

WHEN one returns to view the scenes
   That made and left him happy-hearted,
What if he find the prints of time,
   And mourn the wonted charm departed ?
Relentless time is all the while
   Our hearts from early loves estranging,
The pageant like a picture moves,
   And all the world is changing, changing !

Look up, look up ! for there's a world
   Unknown to care, undimmed by sorrow,
Where all that's bright and fair to-day
   Is full as bright and fair to-morrow.
A world, a home, whose blissful scenes
   Their light forecast in sacred story ;
Be that our rest, to change no more,
   Except from glory unto glory.

6

ATHANASIAN HYMN.

LOVE TO CHRIST.

I GIVE my love to Christ,
  Who gave his love for me,
In walks of sorrow numberless,
  And on the fearful tree.

I tell my love to Christ,
  Who thought of such as I,
In all his happy moments here,
  And asks for love's reply.

I breathe my love to Christ,
  And kneeling hide my face;
How could I make his glory naught,
  And sin against his grace?

I send my love to Christ,
  Who keeps my house above,
And beautifies it while I wait
  The message of his love.

O ye who fly between,
  And ye who journey home,
Angels and saints, convey my love,
  And tell it till I come.

SLEEPING AND WAKING.

My wife had left her home to seek
The glow I worshiped in her cheek,
Like Persian old; my sky had paled;—
A letter every day I mail'd,
And often said, in cheerful vein,
"The baby slept all night again."

All hallow'd by her tears and prayers
He staid with me, it lessen'd cares.
If he, the nestling, slept, I knew
My dove would slumber sweetly too;
And so I wrote her now and then
"The baby slept all night again."

One morn he languish'd at my side
Death-sick, and with the day he died,
And day with him. It was my will
That she I loved be happy still.
So wrote I in my wonted strain
"The baby slept all night again."

But when, in turn, she fondly wrote,
Her pet names using in her note,
With artless talk about the bed
Of him who slept so cold and dead,
I sat the bitter truth to pen,
"He sleeps to wake no more again."

And when upon my breast she lay,
And sobbed her precious bloom away,
And grief met grief, while of the dead
We thought, within his narrow bed,
I said, and saw it ease her pain,
"He wakes, to sleep no more again."

6*

PLEDGED.

THIS is New Year's Day; but flowers
As by miracle are ours;
Love has come with vernal powers.

If the angels sang the warning,
Earth, new-born, their skies adorning,
Or if warblings greet the morning,

Planet of our love so new,
Morn of love so bright in dew,
Hear a song of welcome too:

At God's summons first upspringing,
To his ark its air-way winging,—
Thus begins and ends our singing.

He that with a holy love
Did his beauteous church approve,
And her coming waits above,—

He, the cherish'd bride possessing,
Gave the type and gave the blessing,
Naught of wedded love repressing.

By thy hand that arch'd the heaven,
Spread the light with colors seven,
To the heart its pulse was given;

And the love thence emanating,
Sweetly, strangely operating,
Is of thine approved creating.

Ours to thee we early bring;
Sanctify the offering
For the honor of our King.

Through creation's wondrous plan
In advance love's shadow ran,
Till love came at last with man.

Forms of love the woods were gracing,
Ivy green the oak embracing,
And their leaves soft interlacing.

Hark! the nest-concealing spray
Trembles with a roundelay;
Thus love's season glides away.

Lured by skies and breezes loviug,
Waves apart of late were roving;
Two in one they now are moving,—

Blended on life's boundless ocean,
Fleeting with a joyful motion,
Overpouring with devotion.

With electric love united,
Our enraptured souls are lighted,
By the purple spark ignited.

Is it spark from Eden's ashes
Fires my Eva's cheek and flashes
From beneath her pendent lashes?

Or that shines in skies afar,
Lucid Hope's new kindled star,
Through the door of heaven ajar?

Love can brave the fate's displeasure,
Turn the sable night to azure,
And with flowers crown the glacier.

Jesus unto manhood grown
Trod a pathway woe-bestrown,
Trod it weary and alone.

They for whom his mercy flows,
Overprest with human woes,
On love's bosom may repose.

He, with heart the tenderest,
While around him men were blest,
Had not where his head to rest.

Thou, who must such love forego,
In this wilderness below,
To redeem our souls from woe,—

Thou who hast fulfill'd my prayers
For the one my love that bears
Training for me unawares,

Bless our altar, ever vernal,
Keep us twain in bonds eternal,
Rising to our home supernal.

JANUARY 1st, 18—

MERRILY THE LEAVES FALL.

WRITTEN IN THE FALL OF 1862, IN THE TIME OF THE DRAFTING.

MERRILY the leaves fall;
Falleth so man withal,
Dancing down, glancing down,
In his rags, in his crown.
Sooner frosted at the top,
Lower leaves later drop.
Underneath is room for all;
Merrily, merrily the leaves fall.

Merrily the leaves fall,
Yesternight smitten all,
Racing down, chasing down.
Leaf of red, or leaf of brown,
Holding, doubtful, to the tree,
Join the army of the free.

List ye now while suns are warm,
Or be drafted by the storm;
Do not fear; volunteer;
Take the leap; for the brave are muster'd here.

Merrily the leaves fall,
And to those below they call,—
Let us do the Master's will,
His enlistment to fulfill.
Here we come, glittering host,
Take us to your holocaust.
Leaf of gold and leaf of fire,
Willingly, sacrificed, we expire.

Merrily the leaves fall,
And to those above they call,—
Come ye all, welcome here,
For the God of the year
Loves the beautiful and good,
Takes the bravest of the wood.
All are his; greater price
Does he set on the willing sacrifice.

Merrily the leaves fall,
And to one another call,—

Sweet to live, sweet to die,
Sweeter yet to live on high,
Where our essence, by the breeze
Taken from among the trees,
Carried in a second birth
Higher than the trees of earth,
Lovely shines, softly bright,
In the cloud, full of light.
What is best is best for all;
Merrily, merrily the leaves fall.

FOR A DAY, AND FOR EVER.

Roses visit but a day ;
Sunsets to the rainbows say,
We must go, we cannot stay ;
Back to heaven they troop away.

Beauty unto woman given,
Sooner than the tints of even,
Sooner than the colors seven,
Oft is taken back to heaven.

Love I much thy beauty rare,
Love I more thy mind so fair,
Love thy heart beyond compare,
Heart, that time can never wear.

7

WOMAN'S WAY.

FOND youth, she knows how far to go
Whose acts appear to say thee no;
For love controls her wilful curve,
So proudly verging to reserve.
Though high thy standing in the schools,
And versed in analytic rules,
Thou ne'er hast learn'd in chart to lay
The scollop curve of woman's way.
For she to man is like the flight
On waters smooth of missile light.
A lengthen'd curve; it bends, it dips,
Just touches, and away it skips.
What bold reaction, grace, and pride!
The wooing stream has passage wide.
Yet to a stronger charm submiss,
It comes again the wave to kiss,
And goes and comes with shorter leap;
Then sinks embosom'd in the deep.

ROSE, SHE LIVED AS ROSES LIVE.

" Rose, elle a vécu ce que vivent les roses,
  L'espace d'un matin."
                    [*Inscription on a Young Lady's Tombstone, Paris.*]

" Rose, she lived as roses live,
      But a morn."
Sorrow long in story brief;
Graver, write it deep, for grief
Such as this is never worn.
Death has snatch'd the flower and leaf,
But my heart he left, the thief,
      On a thorn.

Rose, as roses drink the dew,
      Shall receive
Tears, which daily we renew,
      As we grieve.
But she needs them now no more;
'Tis for us the clouded year,
As in mourning mantled o'er,
      When it weeps,

Stays, and once again will pour
On her grave the frequent tear,
    Where she sleeps.

Rose, where roses go she knows,
    In July,
When the sun-god blazes high,
And his beams like nets he throws,
All their sweetness to inclose,
    For the sky,—
Drinks the dewy fragrance up,
Takes the nectar and the cup.
If to follow thee, my Rose,
    I would try,
Something blinds my tearful eye.

Rose, when roses come she knows,
    And I know.
When the sun-god northward goes,
He the laughing spring bestows;
In the tinted sunny rain,
Will he give them back again.
    Hasten June!
Hasten more the time, the time,
When in her immortal prime,

She will come and never go;
Be it soon!
I am hasting thither, Rose,
Pacing with the flying sun,
Wishing till his work is done.

7*

IN HEAVINESS.

WHILE a moon is waning,
There's a hurricane of sighs,
　There's a long day's raining,
Vented from men's hearts and eyes.

　　Sorrow's tear
Is the world express'd in brief;
　　A bright sphere,
But full charged with human grief.

　　Nay, too sad
Are the thoughts such verse engenders ;
　Brighter visions may be had,
Better tidings ean be told ;
Skies are breaking, and behold !
　To allure us all its splendors
Heaven's gateway doth unfold,
　Where the sun at evening renders
Clouds around it Alps of gold.

Wherefore gazing into heaven?
   Angels close beside thee stand.
Those whom thou hast weeping given
   Unto God, at his command,
   Shall return an angel band.

Dust, in beauteous combinations,
   Wins our love and steals our trust;
Hope relies on what foundations
   When the dust returns to dust?

Tell me not the tear of grief
May express the world in brief.
   Not the tear;—
But its pictured fount, the eye,
   A bright sphere,
   When the tear that sped across it
Has gone glittering by,
   Is our world as God can cause it,
   Of creation's wealth the closet
Upward turning to the sky,
Soul and love within, and nigh
Unto Immortality.

THE RICHMOND MARTYRS.

WHAT grief is ours, what vengeance thine, O
    Lord !
  For thousands brave, in ghastly prisons laid,
  With cruel hunger faint, till it be stay'd
By death, long wish'd for by the early sword !
Our loved ones languish, while there stands a
    board
  For those who sacrifice them to their hate,
  And want and woe prepare, and call it fate.
Though hell hath wrought it, 'tis by hell ab-
    horred,
  But not in Richmond, where the souls of men
Are sold for money, or a loaf of bread,
And woman's pity is dried up and dead.
  The tiger cometh to his savage den
To work no lengthen'd torture, such as this,
Whose haunt alone is treason's foul abyss.

THE CHILDREN'S PANEL.

.

THE CHILDREN'S PANEL.

LUCY.

Love for all will stronger prove,
When a floweret goes with love.
There was not a village dame
Cared for flowers when Lucy came.
As their mothers did without them,
Knew not very much about them,
As their fathers' thoughts were bent
On the dollar, dime, and cent,
On the use of things and duty,
Not on ornament and beauty,
All, in course of time, had grown
Quite as flowerless as a stone.

Yonder comes a trim bouquet,
Lucy's gift to Mrs. Gray.

Mrs. Gray is at the door;
Nothing could have pleased her more;
Takes her specs from off the shelf;
"La! I fear you've robbed yourself!"
Then she wonders where they grew;
"I have raised them; you can too;
Here is ground; the sun and showers
Come and go and give us flowers."
Thus she went about the place,
With I know not what of grace,
Cheerful words upon her lips,
Giving seeds and giving slips,
And a bunch of flowers taking,
New desires and joys awaking.

Soon there came to every door
Flowers, the jewels of the poor.
They are rich who happy are;
When the sky shall want a star,
When the earth its flower shall need,
Then will all be poor indeed.

Lucy knew the art of arts,
The unfolding of close hearts.

Now the men a pleasure found
Turning up the mellow ground,
Putting first of all in order
Something for a flower border ;
And the children too would take
Each a part for Lucy's sake.

Many floral gifts she had,
Gifts that made the giver glad.
Seem'd it that the roses threw
Incense to her as they grew.
Seem'd it that the very sod
Came to blossoms where she trod.

Flowerets spring ; our spirits rise
With them nearer to the skies.
Petals open ; love expands,
Self unfolds its narrow bands.

Lesson wise for age and youth,—
In the beautiful is truth ;
In refinement pleasures lie
All unknown to passers-by.

All that tends to render dear
Home to weary children here,
May prepare them more to prize
Home beyond the sunny skies.

Happy village! from thy day
There has passed a cloud away,
And a brightness from above
To the cottage comes in love.

Satan came and turn'd an Eden
To a desert; but the maiden,
Kindness beaming in her eyes,
Made the waste a paradise.

THE YOUNG PAINTER.

Come, beautiful colors, come !
They tell me you live in the sun ;
he paper is all too white, and the picture waits
    to be done ;
With jolly old red
To march at your head,
O won't we all have fun !

You may go, if you will, by-and-by,
To paint the clouds in the sky,
But come ye again at night, ere the rockets begin
    to fly ;
Then turn with the wheels,
And throw up your heels,
And go out all at once, —— so sly !

Last Sunday I must not play,
And they put my brushes away ;
But I saw you at church in a pew, on bonnets
    and dresses so gay ;

And I thought the man said,
"What a beautiful red,
When the world is afire one day!"

I have a bright-spotted shell,
And I heard a sweet lady tell,
That the noise so soft within is a voice from the
ocean's swell.
But I rather think
That the azure and pink
Do whisper, from heaven it fell.

Come, beautiful colors, come!
And finish my soldier and drum;
The rainbows have faded away, and the butter-
flies all are numb;
The flowers are dead,
And the birds are fled;
Then make my house your home.

STORY OF PICKLE GREEN.

COME, let us hear the Flower Queen
The story tell of Pickle Green.
His mother Cucumber had said
He must not leave the garden bed.
But silly pickles love to sneak,
And play around at hide and seek ;
For you must know that naughty vines
Were never planted in the signs.
When Pickle left his mother's door,
And stray'd away a yard or more,
Along the fence he softly stepp'd,
And up between the boards he crept.
He look'd and saw a field beyond,
And lilies, sleeping in a pond.
Said he, "To-night the moon is low ;
To-morrow I will further go."
But ere he sought to travel back,
The rogue had grown and fill'd the crack ;

8*

And morning show'd a sad mishap,
Poor Pickle fasten'd in a trap !
High up among the weeds he grew,
Tortured and pinch'd almost in two,
Just like a wasp with little waist,
Or city lady tightly laced,
Or saddle-bags, the horse astride,
All puffing out on either side.
And when the suns of summer burn'd,
And Pickle Green to yellow turn'd,
The neighbors came to see the sight,
But none could help him in his plight.

Take warning all who truant play,
And loving parents disobey ;
And learn from Pickle's dismal fate
To shun the prison's iron grate.

ALL RIGHT!

O the words are good and strong,
  As you hear them in the cars,
As through life you move along,
  Fearless of its shocks and jars.
We are all in running order,
  Play is fair and honor's bright;
And we signal with our banner,
  All right! all right!

Were we made to fly with wings,
  We would rather be the lark
Than the bat that never sings,
  Flying crooked in the dark.
Could there ever be a window
  In our breasts, not for light,
But for eyes, may they find it
  All right! all right!

THE OPOSSUM.

Run for life, opossum,
　　Like a startled deer;
Chase him, catch him, toss him
　　To the basket here.

Presto ! see him tumble
　　From the broken stump;
Now he's more than humble,—
　　Lifeless as a lump.

Well, it is a wonder
　　Death should come so soon,
Like a clap of thunder
　　From the sun at noon.

Touch him, poke him, shake him,
　　Cunning piece of clay;
Nothing will awake him—
　　Till we go away.

Notice every feature,
   What a look of death!
Tell us, artful creature,
   How to hold the breath.

Dost thou know 'tis human
   Thus to make believe?
Was it man or woman
   Taught thee to deceive?

When again thou learnest,
   Here is knowledge rare,—
Death will come in earnest,
   Fellow, and not spare.

THE SNOW FORT.

First of all, a little ball;
Things the greatest once were small;
Let it travel through the snow;
As we roll it, let it grow.
Warmer work by-and-by,
When you hear the battle-cry.
Work away! call it sport?
This is war! Hurry up, to the fort!

Move along, ball of snow,
Ever gaining as you go,
Never, never coming back,
Nevermore on your track.
Such is youth,—those who care
Let them seek a lesson there.
Life is moving, melting—no!
Roll along! ever gaining as you go.

In the fortress you may stay,
Till the winds are warm, and May
Snows its blossoms on the wall.
Move along, tardy ball!

Otherwise must you die
Where the grass is dead and dry.
O how sweet! then to rest,
And to melt, with a blossom on your breast.

Block to block, and ball to ball,
Upward grows the battle-wall.
Old Gibraltar rises grand!
On the ramparts take your stand,
With a stack of balls to throw;
Launch them on the charging foe!
Steady! sooner die than yield;
Sally forth! sweep them, sweep them from the
    field!

O it seems but yesterday,
Since that lovely month of May,
When I wander'd where they fought,
As do kings, forsooth, for naught.
Yonder lies a ridge of snow,
Where the apple blossoms blow.
Cold! it seems to mock the bees
Overhead, as they murmur in the trees.

But that little ridge of snow
Pass'd, as all things do below.

Summers came and went their way ;
Once again there came a May.
But the war-blast call'd to arms !
Banners rose amid alarms ;
Battle-trains to southward dash'd ;
In the sun regimental armor flash'd.

Of the troop that warred in play
Some to battle march'd away,
March'd with iron in their will
And in hand ; companions still ;
Went, and came not back again,
Like the ball on snowy plain ;
Bravely fought, but not in sport,
With a shout, storming now no mimic fort.

Pass they as the wreath of snow,
Where the apple blossoms blow ?
No ; eternal is their fame,
Still on earth their vital flame ;
They a spark, a living glow
To their country's breast bestow.
If she lives, in her they live,
Evermore, who for hers their being give.